The
Self-Publishing Handbook

Five Key Steps to Professionally Publish Your Book

The
Self-Publishing Handbook

Five Key Steps to Professionally Publish Your Book

Brad Pauquette

Columbus Press
P.O. Box 91028
Columbus, OH 43209
www.ColumbusPressBooks.com

Cover Artwork & Design
Columbus Publishing Lab
www.ColumbusPublishingLab.com

Print ISBN 978-1-63337-004-3
E-book ISBN 978-1-63337-010-4

Printed in the United States of America
1 3 5 7 9 10 8 6 4 2

Contents

Introduction

I recently started raising rabbits at my house. They're cute, friendly and delicious. Being the firm believer in the public library that I am, before I bought a single rabbit or looked through the feed aisle at Tractor Supply, I read everything I could on the subject.

By the end of my research, I was more confused than when I started.

Every book was so comprehensive, I couldn't even begin to sort everything out and find what I needed. I have no interest in raising rabbits with pedigrees or showing my rabbit to win awards, I just want big, fat rabbits. I didn't need to know 10,000 different ways to build a rabbit hutch, I needed to know one really good way, with maybe one or two variations and suggestions for adaptations.

What I wanted was one twenty-page manual that included

the basic information I needed to know now to raise rabbits for meat. What I found were 300-page encyclopedias with an overload of information for every situation, circumstance or contingency.

You're reading this book because you're interested in self-publishing. There are 10,000 ways to go about self-publishing a book. I understand that you don't want or need all of those options. So I've laid out one really good way to get the job done, with a few variations and suggestions to account for your unique project, budget and circumstances.

The five steps I've outlined in this book are steps that publishers and book producers can agree are critical to producing a professional book. Every project is unique, and of course there are tons of options that aren't specifically covered by this handbook, but this is a solid, straightforward path that will lead you through producing a great book.

If we're all being honest, we both know that self-publishing can be really bad. We both know authors who have run their books through some kind of electronic mill and come out the other end with something that looks like a book, but shouldn't be a book. What could have been a great book now reads poorly, is full of errors, is awkwardly laid out and uncomfortable to read. But at least it's for sale on Amazon.com.

There's good news though. Self-publishing, when done right, can be an amazing and fulfilling experience. If you commit yourself to producing something great, you can create a book that competes with the latest releases from Harper Collins, and you can keep 100% of the profits!

Over the past six years I've helped lots of people self-publish their books. From *New York Times* bestselling authors to professional athletes, with a lot of computer programmers, work-from-home moms and accountants in between. I know what it takes to make self-publishing work.

The truth is, most self-published books don't sell very well, even if they're done right. But if you want any chance of success at all, you have to start with a good foundation. The foundation for successful self-publishing is built upon professional production standards.

Unfortunately, producing a great book goes way beyond the manuscript. You need more than great words, you also need your book to be readable, error-free and attractive to buyers.

To produce a great book, we're going to emulate the steps and roles that a traditional publisher employs.

The publishing industry is an old industry (books are one of the oldest mass-produced products in the world), and while there's still a lot of vocabulary from the old days used, the industry has continued to adapt. Book publishers can now produce books at a higher quality and a lower cost than ever before.

Book publishers have continued to experiment and evolve. They've gotten rid of some old jobs and added some new ones. Today, every traditionally published book goes through an important series of production steps. Every step is guaranteed to increase the quality (and profitability) of the book, or the publisher wouldn't do it.

Granted, we don't want to be traditional publishers. There's a lot wrong with that industry. But we can learn the lessons that the publishing industry has spent centuries and billions of dollars perfecting.

The professional book production process includes five critical steps, which will be explained one-by-one in more detail. If you follow each of these steps, you will produce a high quality book.

No one can guarantee that you'll sell a lot of books, but I can guarantee that if you don't produce a professional quality book, you probably won't sell any copies at all. Follow these five steps and you'll have a foundation for success that will make your book attractive to bookstores and readers. With a high quality book, you'll have a springboard for your marketing and networking to take off, and you might just have a chance at great success.

Self-publishing the right way does require some money. However, for those strapped for cash, I have provided do-it-yourself tips for each step. The results won't be the same as if you can hire professional editors and designers to do things right, but you'll still be head-and-shoulders above your self-published peers. At the very least, this handbook should help you decide which tasks you can do yourself, and the ones for which you'll need to find a little money.

If you're using a self-publishing service (AuthorHouse, Lulu, CreateSpace, Xlibris, etc.), note that many of their packages don't include all five of these steps. These services have a tendency to focus on one thing—cover design. Use this handbook to make sure that you're receiving all of the processes you need to produce a great book.

With each step, I also provide some information about the way that my company, Columbus Publishing Lab, does things. This handbook isn't designed to be a solicitation to use our services, but I do know that we do things right. Frankly, I started my company because I was fed up with seeing services like the ones mentioned above rip off hard-working authors by producing crap materials at exorbitant prices. If you'd like to use Columbus Publishing Lab, we'd love to speak with you. But more importantly, you can use this information as a standard to which you can compare the services you're receiving or considering from a different company.

If you prefer to manage the project yourself, this handbook also provides helpful tips for hiring freelancers, contractors and consultants. All prices provided as examples are based on the 2014 market in Columbus, Ohio, a medium-sized city, and are best applied to a 50,000 to 80,000 word fiction novel. Specific prices may need to be adjusted based on the length of your book and your local market, as well as for inflation.

Self-publishing is a continually evolving marketplace. Every day there are new opportunities for authors interested in self-publishing. Most of them are great ways to throw away your hard-earned cash, but occasionally something good comes along. This handbook does not take into account every path that you may find.

If you commit yourself to these five steps, you'll produce a professional book and you'll be on solid footing. Self-publishing is always a risky business venture, but if you follow this path, you'll have a firm foundation.

Getting Started

It's time for the self-publishing industry to change. The demand for self-published books and the technology to produce and sell them is finally leveling out. Self-publishers are in a unique position to produce better books than ever before at a reasonable cost, and to have fair access to mainstream markets.

There is no reason that self-publishers shouldn't be producing books that are as good as their traditionally published counterparts.

If more self-publishers commit themselves to producing professional books, the publishing industry as a whole will change. You owe it to yourself to do things right, and to produce a book that's objectively as good as its traditionally published peers.

Publishers and professional book producers use five critical steps to produce quality books. Thanks to evolving technology and a changing marketplace for independent providers, you now have access to the same professionals and processes that traditional publishers use. As a self-publisher, you can effectively replicate the same production process as a traditional publisher. You can build an amazing, professional book of the same quality that the bigger publishers are producing, and you can do it much cheaper and faster than they can.

The book creation process includes five key steps. If you incorporate all five of these steps into your book production process, you will produce a great book.

Step 1: Development Editing - The first step is developmental editing—getting objective, third party feedback on your manuscript and making big changes. No matter how good you think your manuscript is, it can be better. No book goes to print through a traditional publisher without getting torn apart several times and stitched back together.

Step 2: Copy Editing - The second step is copy editing— standardizing language and punctuation usage, formatting your manuscript to a professional style guide and correcting any mistakes on a line-by-line basis. If you want bookstores and readers to take your book seriously, you must prove that you understand professional standards.

Step 3: Interior Design - The third step is the interior design of the book, where your book is designed to fit into a printed size of your choice with comfortable margins and a consistent visual presentation. In this step, your book is also prepared for distribution as an e-book.

Step 4: Proofreading - The fourth step is proofreading. This is our last chance to catch any minor mistakes. It could be things the copy editor missed (there are always a few), or perhaps during the design process some incongruities appeared. In any case, the proofreading step finds and corrects any remaining minor errors.

Step 5: Cover Design - The final step is cover design, where we put together a fantastic cover that will attract buyers and reinforce the themes of your book.

Your book is ready for the printer!

This is the process that even the biggest traditional publishers use, and they use it because it's efficient and effective. You can replicate this process, and if you commit yourself to a professional process you can expect great results. Some things you'll be able to do yourself, and other things you'll need to hire out. But the one thing I hear self-publishers say more than anything else is, "I wasted hundreds of frustrating hours trying to produce my book. I should have spent some money and done it right."

Whether you take care of each of these steps yourself, or use a self-publishing service with an "all-inclusive" package, with this handbook you'll be equipped to make sure that you're creating a fantastic book. Along the way, you may find that some of those packages aren't so "all-inclusive" after all.

Welcome to the Business

Before you start researching self-publishing, finish your manuscript. Don't use preparedness as an excuse to procrastinate finishing your book. Until (and unless) your book is done, you've got no business doing anything else.

Once you declare the manuscript finished, the artist-writer inside of you exits the building, and it's time for the business person to come out.

The hardest part about self-publishing is all of the different hats you'll have to wear. You're no longer just a writer, you're also an editor, a project manager, a book publicist and so much more. Most importantly, you're now a business person.

Whether you only intend to self-publish this one book, or you have lots in mind for down the road, you are starting a small publishing company. The best way to be successful is to know which hat you're wearing at all times, and to do it to the best of your ability.

When it's time to wear the business hat, remember three very important things: product, objectivity and capital.

Businesses create products for a market. Sometimes the product is a service, sometimes it's an idea, sometimes it's a spatula, and sometimes it's a book, but the core of all business is to produce a product and to find consumers who need it. Once you begin your journey of self-publication, your book is no longer a work of art that you suffered to bare to the world, it is now a product. This is the hardest thing you'll have to accept as a writer, and this is why so many self-publishers fail. Your job is now to produce the best product that you can, and to find customers who want to buy it, end of story.

Objectivity is related. Normally in publishing, there's a healthy contest between the publisher and the author. The publisher wants to do everything for profit, and the author wants to do everything for art. Normally they meet somewhere in between the two poles, but much closer to the publisher's side of things. As a self-publishing author, you need to contend for both sides of the debate, and ultimately, you need to let the profit-driven publisher side win.

You need to fall out of love with your work, and get real about turning it into the best product. Your book might be very good, but it's not yet the best that it can be. No book leaves the author's hands fully formed. It needs to be cleaned up, groomed and improved.

Capital does matter. "You've got to spend money to make money," as they say. There will be circumstances where a lot of time, willingness to learn and resilience will get the job done in place of money, but there will be times when you'll simply need a little cash.

The more cash you bring into the game, the easier your job becomes and the higher your chances of success. You can successfully self-publish with almost no cash, but it will be more difficult. Don't fall into the trap of believing that the winner is the guy who wanted it most. A lot of the times, the winner is the guy who brought the largest stack to the table.

Your Pathways

Self-publishing is any publishing process by which you, as the author, pay for or are the sole motivator of the production and sale of the book. This includes paying for a service to publish your book, or using a "free" service to publish your book. Unless there is an editor who has selected your book from a large list of candidates, and a company that is going to be investing a large amount of cash in the production and distribution of your book, you are a self-publisher.

As a self-publisher, there are three major pathways available to you:

Vanity Publishing – This is where you pay a "publisher" a large sum of money to treat you as if they selected your book for publication. They'll take your manuscript (including the rights), run it through their book-production machine, and sell your book on your behalf. It'll cost a lot of money and you'll make almost nothing off of the books that you sell, but it'll be hands-off, and your more gullible friends will believe that you're a legitimately published author.

Self-Publishing Service – These are services like Lulu.com. You maintain more of the rights and the profits than you would through a vanity publisher, and you exert more control over the production process. In most cases, you'll select a package that includes editing and design services, maybe some marketing services as well, pay a lump sum and they'll produce your book. This is a mixed bag. Some of these services are very good and charge a fair amount, others will get tricky with the contract you sign and produce poor work. The advantage is that it's easy. Just like vanity publishing, you deliver a manuscript and let the machinery work its magic. You don't need to know anything to complete the project, you just need to pay the fees and trust the company you've contracted.

Manage your own Project – This is the fun one, and this is what most successful self-publishers do. It also comes with the most risk. With this option, you'll find and hire your own editors, designers and marketing services one at a time, and lead yourself through the self-publication process. With this option, you'll typically get the best results for the lowest cost, and you will maintain 100% of the profits for yourself. The downside is that it's difficult to do the first time, you'll make a lot of mistakes and there are plenty of headaches.

There is a fourth option, which is a hybrid of a self-publishing service and managing your own project. This is what you can do through CreateSpace and Columbus Publishing Lab. You maintain all rights and control of your project, but all of the services that you may need are available to you. This saves you the trouble of finding a book cover designer or a qualified developmental editor (and messing with freelancers) on your own. Instead, a reputable company provides all of the functions and people you may need, and stands behind the work. Typically, the cost is about the same as managing your own project, because the company is working in higher quantities and can therefore contract these services on your behalf cheaper than you could go out and hire individual freelancers one at a time. The turnaround time will be much faster as well.

With the hybrid approach, at the end of the day you pick and choose what you need. If you have a designer or an editor that you'd like to use instead of the one offered by the company, you're free to do that, and the company will still help you distribute the book to retailers. You get the ease of use and quick production time of a self-publishing service, but you get the great product and control that you would if you managed the project yourself.

This handbook will be most helpful to the self-publisher who intends on managing her own project, or using a hybrid company.

Defining Success

When I talk about "successful" self-published books, I don't necessarily mean titles that have sold a million copies and landed on *The New York Times* best-seller list. When I say success, I mean one thing: The book exceeded the author's goals.

Not everybody sets out to make a gazillion dollars. When I self-published my novellete, *Sejal: The Walk for Water*, I didn't set out to make any money at all. I simply wanted to get the book into circulation and to educate more Americans about the water crisis in India.

So don't set out to sell a million books. If it happens, that's fantastic, but in reality it's a ridiculous goal and practically impossible. Even if you're setting out to make money, set a reasonable goal. When in doubt, I recommend five thousand books as an ambitious sales number over two years.

At 5,000 books, you're going to have a solid platform for your second book. If you approach a traditional publisher and say, "I self-published my first book and sold 5,000 copies," they'll suddenly become more interested in your work.

Two years is important. Book campaigns are two-year investments in the publishing industry. Don't expect the books to fly off the shelves in the first three months. Most authors will experience a sales surge in the first month, mostly due to friends and family. Month two will tank, and from there your job is to sell more books than you did the month before, for twenty-four months in a row.

At 5,000 books, you've easily recovered whatever you spent on the book production, you should have recovered your marketing cost and you're in a comfortable position to either take a paycheck or reinvest in your book.

Manage your expectations, and define your success as something obtainable before you begin. It's unlikely that you're going to end up a millionaire, but in two years you could be a person who makes money by writing books, and that would be pretty cool.

The truth is that most self-publishers are not successful. That's because most great writers are not very good business people, and most people who can take care of business are not great writers. This is compounded by the fact that most self-publishers expect to see their name in *The New York Times* next week, and to be on *Good Morning America* the week after that.

You've reached this step because you believe you've written a great and valuable book. The key to your success will be to step back from your work, to transform yourself into a business person and to set a reasonable benchmark for success.

Your manuscript is done. It's time to put on the publisher hat and to focus on producing the best product possible.

Questions & Answers

Before we begin the production process, there are a few questions we'll have to answer.

Paperback or Hardback?

The first step is to decide what type of book you want to produce. Unless you're working with a budget of more than $50,000 (in which case, this is not the right handbook for you), it almost always makes sense to start by producing a paperback book.

Hardback books are affordable if you're producing 10,000+ units. Below that, the economy of scale just doesn't work. In addition to the printing cost, hardbacks cost twice as much to ship.

In most cases, you'll find it a lot easier to sell a paperback for $12 to $20 than a hardback which you'll have to price at $28 to $35.

For the remainder of this handbook, we'll assume that you've chosen to produce a paperback book. If you're planning on producing a hardback book, you'll need to adapt some of the design information.

If you're choosing an e-book only route, you'll also find tips for that. But much of the process will remain the same.

Should I Produce an E-Book Too?

Yes! As long as you know up front that you're intending on producing an e-book, it will add less than 10% to the total production cost. And your base of potential readers will grow exponentially!

For books produced by Columbus Press, my independent publishing company, we typically sell half e-books and half print books, split right down the middle. You don't want to lose half of your potential audience to save 10% on the production cost.

The great thing about e-books is that once the files are produced, there's virtually no additional cost. You can sell four copies of your e-book or 40,000 copies, and your only investment was the tiny increase in initial cost of the book design. In business we have a technical term for that, it's called a "win-win."

Make sure that your designers know up front that you want to produce an e-book.

Who's the Publisher?

This is a question that a lot of self-publishers get hung up on. What name will appear on the back of the book?

You have three options—your name, the name of a company you start, or the name provided by your self-publishing service.

Many self-publishers simply use their own name. The back of the book and the copyright page say "Published by Sally Jones." There's nothing wrong with that, it's cheap and easy.

Some self-publishers choose to file as an LLC with their state. Creating an LLC is easy. It'll take you an hour and cost about $100. You can register as anything you want, "Sally Jones Publishing LLC" or "Big Boss Press, Ltd." The advantage to creating an LLC is that it professionalizes your book (it looks more like a traditionally published book), it provides a financial barrier (the book is owned and produced by the LLC, not by you personally), and it may make your taxes a little less complicated (or not). As an LLC, you can open a business bank account and keep your self-publishing venture separate from your personal finances. If you have more questions about creating an LLC, your state's Small Business Administration or Secretary of State can help.

The third option is to use what your self-publishing service provides. So the back of the book will say "CreateSpace" or "Xlibris" as the publisher. This is fine. The only disadvantage is that it will be obvious that you self-published, and in some cases, you may forfeit some claim to ownership of the title. Some self-publishing services will allow you to use your own name instead of theirs, but some require you to use their name as the publisher.

At Columbus Publishing Lab, clients can either bring their own name (their personal name or the name of their LLC), or we have two imprints that they can use—Proving Press or Boyle & Dalton. Either way, the client maintains all rights to their title.

You'll need a few things before you can publish your book…

The ISBN

Your book will need an ISBN, which stands for International Standard Book Number. Every book sold at a bookstore has an ISBN.

A company called Bowker administrates all of the ISBNs in the United States. You can learn more at MyIdentifiers.com. The price of an ISBN fluctuates based on how many you buy. I recommend that you buy a block of ten ISBNs, which currently costs $250. If you're producing a paperback and an e-book, you'll probably need at least two ISBNs. The alternative is to buy them individually for $125 each, but you can do the math there. At least with ten, you'll have some options.

If you use a self-publishing service, they'll likely be able to provide you with an ISBN or you can bring your own. The good thing about using theirs is that they can buy them in massive bulk, so it's usually cheaper. Sometimes they'll give it to you for "free," other times they'll charge you for it, but either way it will probably cost less than $125.

The disadvantage to using an ISBN that someone else provides to you is that whoever registers the ISBN will be the official publisher of record for all eternity. So if you get your ISBN from CreateSpace, the official registration will say "CreateSpace" instead of "Tom Jones." If you're self-publishing, but planning on making it appear as if you were independently published (or started your own publishing company), this will blow your cover. Some self-publishing services will allow you to purchase and bring your own ISBN in lieu of using theirs.

In 2007, ISBNs switched from a ten digit number to a thirteen digit number. With the influx of published books, we were running out of numbers. You may see references to ISBN-10 and ISBN-13, but this distinction is largely irrelevant. Today, you can only purchase ISBN-13s, so don't let these terms distract you. ISBN-10s will still work if you have them, but if you purchase new ISBNs now, you'll only have ISBN-13s available to you.

Each unique ISBN can only be used once. If a book undergoes a revision and a new edition is released, a new ISBN must be issued. You can make minor grammatical changes without getting a new ISBN.

The Barcode

Where do I get that cool UPC thing for the back of my book? The barcode on the back of your book, so that retailers can scan it, is also sold by Bowker at MyIndentifiers.com. It will cost you $25 per barcode. The good news is that your e-book doesn't need one (duh, right?).

If you use a self-publishing service, it's the same story as the ISBN. You can set it up yourself or use theirs. There is no bulk discount for barcodes, so you'll have to pay for it. But most likely it's factored into the cost of the ISBN or the design.

When you create your barcode, you should download it from MyIndentifiers.com as a PDF and an EPS (the option to do this will be obvious when you set up the barcode). You'll need to provide both of these things to your cover designer.

Book barcodes are different from other commodities in that the price of the book is actually encoded into the barcode. That means you'll need to know the price of your book before you create a barcode, and if you change your price at some point, you'll need to pay for another barcode and update your book cover. See the chapter on "Pricing Your Book" before you create a barcode.

The Library of Congress Number (LCCN)

How do you get that cool LCCN number for the copyright page? It's easy and free to setup.

Go to www.loc.gov/publish/pcn/ and you can create a free

account. Make sure to follow all of the instructions.

After the book is produced, you'll need to mail a copy of the printed book to the Library of Congress. But that's the only real cost.

You don't really need this number, but it can be helpful, especially if you want libraries to carry your book. Since the LCCN is free, why not?

Fun Fact: LCCN used to stand for Libary of Congress Card Number, back when libraries used the card catalog system (remember the tiny drawers with all of the little cards?). Now that everything's digital, LCCN stands for Library of Congress Catalog Number.

U.S. Copyright

When to copyright your book is always a good question. It's a better question for a lawyer, but here are a few simple guidelines.

If your book changes, you'll need to apply for a new copyright. So if you apply for a copyright for your manuscript before you begin the production process and then work with an editor and make changes, you'll need a new copyright. The cost of a copyright isn't high, it can just be a pain to file.

Your work is your indisputable intellectual property as soon as it exists in a permanent form (like on a piece of paper). The official U.S. Copyright just helps you prove in court when your work existed. So if someone copies you, you can show this piece of paperwork from the government that proves that your work existed before theirs did.

So the copyright helps you prove things. But it doesn't make your work any more or less your work.

Many authors are worried about their work or idea being stolen by a designer or editor during the production process. I have never seen this happen. It's certainly not impossible, but in my experience, it's not a high risk. Professional editors and designers make a lot more money (and preserve their reputation) by producing your work. Stealing your manuscript and then trying to sell it themselves would be a long shot at best, and scarcely worth sacrificing a guaranteed paycheck.

I've seen many clients never officially copyright their work (even after beginning to sell it). That's probably not a good approach, but the point is that you have a lot of flexibility. Figure out what makes sense to you, and don't stress out about the copyright.

Most authors choose to copyright their work when they're ready to print. In the cases that I've seen, this works well and saves some time and money. Copyright is a complex issue, so if you have more questions, you should research it and speak to an attorney.

You don't need to have all of these things squared away

before you begin the editing process. You'll need the ISBN, the LCCN and the publisher's name before you get to the interior design, and you'll need the barcode before you complete the cover design. The copyright is up to you.

Armed with this information, you're ready to begin the book production process.

Step One
Developmental Editing

"The End." Your book is done now, right? Ship it off to CreateSpace and see your name on Amazon! Not so fast...

Developmental editing is one of the most frequently overlooked steps in the book design process, yet in the professional publishing world it is one of the most important.

Developmental editing is the process by which you get objective, third party feedback on your manuscript and make big changes. In most cases, this consists of hiring an experienced editor to read your manuscript and to make recommendations on how you can improve it.

In the Publishing Industry

If you were to publish your book traditionally, you would typically endure several rounds of developmental editing. If you're lucky enough to land an agent, typically she will request lots of changes to your manuscript before she begins to contact publishers about your book. In a lot of cases, you may be asked to make huge overhauls to your book three or more times. Delete scenes, add characters, move the end to the beginning—these are all things that may be asked of you.

But wait, you're not done. If you're so lucky as to have your agent successfully sell your book to a publisher, one of the first people you'll meet is your editor. This person is going to start the process all over again. In fact, you may spend up to a year with this person making revision after revision until the book is the best that it can be.

It takes a long time for a book to go from the author's computer to store bookshelves, and most of that process is tied up in developmental editing. Publishers spend a lot of time and money making sure that this step is expertly executed, because it's important. Nobody skips it. From James Joyce to James Patterson to Jim Nobody, if you're published by a traditional publisher, no one walks right to the printer.

If it's that important to publishers, it probably ought to be important to us too, right?

Doing It Professionally

The best option is to hire a professional developmental editor. Developmental editing is a different job from copy editing or proofreading, so it's important to find someone who has this specific skill set. The developmental editor has a special knack for analyzing a manuscript for narrative success as well as marketability, and seeing big picture solutions for reorganizing and adapting the book to make it more successful.

DO NOT hire your church newsletter editor, your eleventh grade English teacher or your friend who never writes an email without a typo for this job. Some of the jobs we'll discuss can be accomplished by the people around you, but this is not one of them.

The cost of developmental editing depends on the quality of the editor, the length of your manuscript and what kind of shape your book is in. For a book that is 50,000 to 80,000 words, you should expect to pay between $500 and $3,000 per edit. In some cases, your book will require more than one round of developmental editing. If you look online, you'll find "average" prices are much higher than this. But that's misinformation perpetuated by the publishing industry. Good editors can and do work faster than what you'll find listed, and the price will be less.

The typical turnaround time for this service should be about three weeks. Note that good editors usually have a backlog of projects, so they may not be able to start right away.

What You Should Expect

In most cases, when the editor is finished, she will return your printed manuscript with notes on every page (called "margin notes"), as well as a report. Your developmental editor should not make changes directly to the manuscript. If they do, you've hired the wrong person. The developmental editor's job is to make recommendations. You're still the writer and it's still your job to implement those suggestions.

Typically, margin notes will focus on specific things on a scene-by-scene level. Are there parts that don't make sense? Is a character confusing or poorly developed? Is a section boring, repetitive or unnecessary? Does the dialogue sound real?

The report that you receive will focus on bigger picture items. Is there a way to reorganize the narrative to reinforce your themes more effectively and make the story more interesting? Is the book as a whole too long or too short? Overall, is it a good read?

At the end of the day, a good editor will tell you a) is this book any good, and b) is there a market for this book. If the editor doesn't answer these questions (or it seems like they're trying to protect your feelings), he's not doing his job.

Developmental editing is the hardest step. The purpose of this step is to identify things that you're not doing very well and to have someone tell you to your face what you can do better. That can be hard for authors to swallow.

Whether you hire your own editor, or go through this phase with a traditional publisher, it's not fun to be told what you've done wrong. But you're not a prodigy, no one is.

Your book can be better. And if you're going to be successful in this highly competitive market, it needs to be better.

Hiring a Developmental Editor

Hiring a developmental editor can be difficult. The Internet is a great place to start. It's always a plus if you can hire someone locally who you can sit down with face-to-face, but this is a specialized skill set, so you may have to look to the nearest big city.

Make sure to interview more than one editor, and avoid choosing based on personality alone. Remember, you want someone who can give you bad news without worrying about your feelings.

A good editor will be able to show you examples of other books he's edited. A good editor will request a sample of your work before giving you an estimate, but when you are given an estimate it will be an exact number with a clearly defined turnaround time, not a ballpark quote. A good editor will be able to tell you exactly what you can expect to get back from him, and when.

There isn't really a rule book for the developmental editor, so your experience can vary. It's a job that everyone does differently, and you're hiring the editor's intuition, which can be difficult to define. Nonetheless, here are some qualities that you'll find among almost all qualified developmental editors:

Qualities of a Good Developmental Editor

- Professional - Is courteous in emails and phone

calls, shows up on time.
- Experienced - Can show you past work, and volunteers examples.
- Precise - When it comes time to give a price, the editor knows what it will cost and how long it will take.
- Listens - It's important that your editor understands your goals. Are you communicating well and is the editor taking the time to listen to you?

There are certainly exceptions to the rule, but here are some warning signs that you may want to interview other candidates:

Warning Signs of a Bad Developmental Editor
- Jack-of-all-trades - Does this person offer everything? Do they want to do your copy editing and proofreading too, or maybe even the design?
- Vague - Do they seem uncertain of how long it may take, how much it might cost or exactly what you'll get back? This is a sign of inexperience.
- Moonlighter - Is this the person's full-time job, or is there something else they'd rather do and they're just trying to make a few bucks on the side? There's certainly some consideration for younger professionals who are trying to make the transition to free-

lancing or full-time editing, but make sure they're passionate about this job and not just trying to make a few more bucks for beer and pizza or to pay down their student loans.

Of course, there are great developmental editors who defy these rules. But it's a good starting point.

A Note About Providing Samples

Most editors will request a sample of your work. Give it to them. Authors are typically worried about someone stealing their work at this stage. But professional editors have too much to lose by stealing your work, and stealing a client's manuscript wouldn't be that profitable. If they seem like a legitimate operation and they ask for a sample of your work, which they should, give it to them.

Always email a sample. State what you're providing in the email and ask the editor to confirm receipt.

"Dear editor,

As requested, here are the first three chapters of my novel *The Long, Hard Road*. Please confirm that you received this."

It's not foolproof, but you've got a paper trail, and you're in good shape.

If you're really worried about it, you can apply for a copyright before interviewing editors. But note that since you'll be making lots of changes, you'll have to get another copyright when it comes time to publish the book.

The Do-It-Yourself Way

Not everyone can afford to hire a developmental editor. That's understandable. Unfortunately, this isn't a job that most authors can ask their spouse, mother, friend or pastor to do for them. In order for developmental editing to work, you need someone who not only has the skill to see your mistakes and what can be improved, but has the stomach to tell you what you've done wrong. Despite their best intentions, I've never met an author who successfully received the right kind of feedback from friends and family.

The best alternative to hiring a developmental editor is to find a good writers' workshop that is committed to providing feedback at a professional level. You're not looking for a writers' group that encourages everyone to follow their dreams and thinks that writing is the most valuable expressive art form, you're looking for a serious collegiate-style critique group that will hold your work to the same standard that a professional publisher would.

If you can't find a qualified critique group in your area, Columbus Creative Cooperative provides a private online feedback forum where you can submit your work and receive valuable feedback. You can find it at www.ColumbusCoop.org.

The disadvantage to a writers' workshop is that it will take a long time to get through your book. Typically, you'll only be able to submit a few chapters at a time. So it may take months or even over a year to get feedback on the full text, and it's unlikely that you'll get the same big picture feedback that you would get from an editor who reads the full text in one sitting.

Nonetheless, getting feedback on a professional level is so important to successfully publishing a great book. If you're on a tight budget, a writers' workshop is the best way to get the job done.

The End of the Road

Sometimes this is the end of the project, and rightly so.

Most of the time the developmental editor will provide suggestions for improvement. But in some cases, he may tell you that your book doesn't have it. Don't take it personally, that's exactly the feedback that you need. It means, "Try again, but don't waste any more time or money on this project."

That feedback hurts. But if you get it, listen. Listen to that advice at this stage, and you can save yourself a lot of trouble. The developmental editor is doing his job. He doesn't want to give you that advice any more than you want to hear it, so take it seriously.

Even if the manuscript as a whole is really bad, most manuscripts have some good qualities that can be worked with and improved to produce a great book. But every once in a while, the only responsible advice to give is, "Scrap this, try again."

The Columbus Publishing Lab Way

At Columbus Publishing Lab we have a team of developmental editors, each suited to a particular set of genres. When you're ready to get honest, objective feedback on your manuscript, we match you with the best editor for the job at a fair, affordable rate.

Due to the large range of cost for developmental editing (depending on the author's requests and the quality of the manuscript), developmental editing is not currently included in any of our self-publishing packages. Each manuscript is considered and quoted on a case-by-case basis to make sure that you, the author, are getting the best service at the fairest price.

All of our editors provide a complete report outlining the manuscript's strengths and weaknesses, and addressing marketability. Editors also return the printed manuscript with margin notes throughout.

We also provide developmental editing services to clients who are interested in taking their book through traditional publishers. It can be a great first step to make sure that your manuscript is in top shape before you approach agents and publishers. As they say, you only get one chance at a first impression.

The Take Away

Every manuscript can be better. It doesn't matter how many times you've run through it yourself, you absolutely need objective, third party feedback that will hold your work to a professional standard. It can be expensive, but it's a worthwhile investment.

Authors who work with an editor usually walk away saying something like, "I'm so glad I did that. I was missing so many obvious ways to make my book better."

Step Two
Copy Editing

Copy editing is the editing that authors are most familiar with. Sometimes called "line editing," this is the process where an editor goes through your manuscript, line-by-line, to conform the text to a style guide (like *The Chicago Manual of Style*), fix grammatical mistakes, correct punctuation errors and make small usage changes (like eliminating repeated words).

When you submit an article to the local paper, or the church newsletter, this is typically the job that the "editor" is doing before your work goes to print.

In the Publishing Industry
Unlike the developmental editor whose work is based primarily on intuition (what would feel better to the reader), the copy editor's job is based entirely on concrete knowledge and facts. Professional copy editors know an ungodly number

of style and grammar rules. Each style guide has thousands of rules, and many copy editors are proficient in multiple style guides.

Their job goes beyond when to write out "ninety-nine" and when to write "99," they also need to know things like whether "turtleneck" is one word or two (it's one), and whether "twentysomethings" needs to be hyphenated (it doesn't). All of this is in addition to the regular punctuation and grammar rules which most of us left in eleventh grade English class.

The copy editor also checks to make sure that "Sarah," a minor character in chapter one, doesn't become "Sara" (no h) in chapter seventeen.

This job may seem unimportant (who really cares if it's "99" or "ninety-nine" after all?), but it is absolutely critical to the professionalism of your book and to your reader's experience. Believe it or not, readers do notice these types of errors, and these errors subconsciously weigh on the narrator's voice and credibility.

Most importantly, there will be obvious grammatical errors in a 70,000 word manuscript. It's important that your work is formatted correctly and error-free.

Traditional publishers spend a lot of money retaining the best copy editors, because they know how valuable this step is to producing quality materials and ultimately how important it is to good sales numbers.

Doing It Professionally

Your best option is to hire a professional, independent copy editor. A professional copy editor will be able to provide excellent results and be able to return your manuscript to you in a short period of time. Unlike a developmental editor who needs time to digest your manuscript and reflect on it, in most cases a copy editor simply needs to move through the manuscript line-by-line until the job is complete.

The cost of a copy editor can vary significantly based on the editor's experience level, the competition in your local market and the quality of your manuscript. Since the editor is making changes directly to the manuscript, there's a big difference between a text that needs corrections to every sentence and one that has a few errors on each page. For a typical 50,000 to 80,000 word manuscript, you should expect to pay between $200 and $1,000.

Copy editing is often something that a self-publishing service, like Columbus Publishing Lab, can provide for significantly less cost than a freelancer can. Simply put, on a project-by-project basis, it's much less expensive to hire a full-time employee (if you can keep them busy) than it is to hire an independent freelancer, who has to do their own accounting, marketing and everything else that comes with running a business. A full-time copy editor can edit 200+ manuscripts per year, while a freelancer (since they need to spend time finding business, running consultations, paying taxes, etc.) would be hard pressed to complete 100 manuscripts per year. If they both want to make the same amount of money, obviously the freelancer needs to receive more per project.

What You Should Expect

In almost all cases, you will need to provide the editor with an editable digital copy of your manuscript, like a Microsoft Word (.doc, .docx) document. Talk to your editor about what file types they accept, and if there's any problem they should be able to help you convert your file to the necessary format.

Most editors will return your manuscript to you in the same file format that you provided it within two to three weeks. Some editors may have a way for you to see what changes they've made, but most will simply provide the final, ready-to-go file to you.

You should expect to receive an exact price for the project before the editor begins. If you use a freelancer, you'll typically be asked to pay about half of the cost up front, with the remainder due upon completion of the project. If you use an established self-publishing service, most will ask for the full project price up front.

Hiring a Copy Editor

Hiring a copy editor is significantly easier than hiring a developmental editor. A classified ad (like on Craigslist.org) may be a good place to start, but it's also likely that you can simply search for a copy editor in your area on Google.

Magazines, newspapers and advertising agencies all need lots of copy editors, so there's usually plenty of experienced individuals available.

You can often find the best deal by looking towards a self-publishing service (like Columbus Publishing Lab) or an author's services company. But there are also plenty of freelance copy editors who can handle your job.

Questions to Ask a Potential Copy Editor

What style guide would you use for my book? - The content of the answer isn't important, but it is important that she can confidently provide a specific answer. All we care about is that the book is professional and consistent throughout, whatever style guide the editor uses to make that happen is up to her. If you ask this question and the editor stares at you blankly, him-haws, or gives you a round-about answer, interview other candidates.

How long will the copy editing process take? - The editor should be able to provide a precise turnaround time. Remember, good editors will have a backlog of projects, so if that's what's increasing the turnaround time, that's OK.

What's your day job? - You're looking for a full-time freelance copy editor, or a person who works as a copy editor for a business during the day and is picking up extra cash with a few projects in their spare time. What you don't want is a bookstore clerk or a college student doing this job on the side. You'll probably get a great price from that person, but poor results, if they ever finish the job at all.

Can I see examples of your work? - An experienced editor will be able to point you to lots of things they've edited. What's the production quality of the samples they provide? Are they nicely produced materials that you'd pay money for, or are they plain paper community newsletters?

How much will this cost? - A good editor will ask for a sample before quoting your copy editing (except sometimes in the case of a self-publishing service). A manuscript with a lot of mistakes will take so much more time than one with very few mistakes. An editor who gives a one-size-fits-all quote based on the word count probably doesn't have a lot of experience, or they're quoting everyone for the worst case scenario.

Of course we're speaking in generalities here, and you'll find lots of exceptions. The answers to these questions should be warning flags, not deal breakers.

The Do-It-Yourself Way

Sometimes, this is a job that a friend can help you with. It's not a job that you can do yourself (we all tend to overlook errors in our own work), but a friend who knows his grammar rules and is willing to spend a lot of time looking things up can help.

It's important to remember that this job is a lot more than just reading the text. In fact, the content is almost completely unimportant. The key is to dissect the work one sentence at a time, to look up any odd words (like "turtleneck," "twenty-somethings" and "OK") and to, most importantly, be consistent from the first page to the last page.

Most people find that even though this step costs a few hundred dollars to hire out, it's well worth it. An experienced copy editor will be able to move through the manuscript literally ten times faster and the results will be noticeably better. But if you decide that you must do this step yourself, and you have a knowledgeable, reliable friend to help, it can be done.

The Columbus Publishing Lab Way

At Columbus Publishing Lab you can purchase copy editing as part of one of our self-publishing packages, or we can quote your manuscript independently.

We'll request an editable copy of your manuscript (like a Microsoft Word .doc or .docx, but whatever you have we can work with) and we'll return your completed manuscript to you, typically within two weeks.

Whether you intend to self-publish your book through Columbus Publishing Lab, or you just need copy editing service before you take the work elsewhere, we're here to help. Our knowledgeable, competent staff will provide excellent work at a great price.

The Take Away

Copy editing is a hard job that takes a special kind of brain. A friend can do it if he really puts a lot of time and effort into it, but most people aren't suited for it.

Don't underestimate the value of effective copy editing. If you read reviews of self-published books on Amazon.com, it won't take long before you find one that has a lower rating because of copy editing errors. I don't know why, but readers do care!

Step Three
Interior Design

You've worked on the content and had the line-by-line errors edited out of your manuscript, now it's time to make it look like a book!

"Interior Design" is the process of taking your manuscript and formatting it with a book design program so that it can be sent to a printer or exported as an e-book. This step is sometimes called "Typesetting" or sometimes just "Design."

This is the step that first-time self-publishers almost always wish they would have sourced to a professional.

Once you start this step, your book is set in stone. The only changes you can make are minor proofreading/typo changes. Make sure your book is ready to go before you begin the interior design.

In the Publishing Industry
In the traditional publishing industry, this process is

nearly invisible to the author. The publisher will simply have it done and then present the final text to the author.

It will be the designer's job to decide fonts, text size, layout and alignment issues. The designer is a trained professional who knows the genre, and is familiar with the requirements of the publisher's printers and e-book markets.

Doing it Professionally

The best way to accomplish this step is to hire a professional book designer. You'll pay between $200 and $1,000 (for a simple text book, no pictures), but it will be well worth it. This is the step that self-publishers are most likely to try to do themselves, but hundreds of frustrating hours later they almost always wish they'd just paid someone a couple hundred dollars to do it for them.

What to Expect

The interior design is typically a hands-off process. Up front, the designer will ask you if there's anything that you like and ask you to provide examples. For instance, you may show them a book in which you really like the title page, another book for the table of contents and another book that you think has great chapter headers.

The designer will want to know who will be printing your book, as this will affect minimum margins, and a lot of other technical details regarding the design. If you're not settled on one, make sure that the designer knows all of the options you're considering.

Finally, your book designer will need to know what size you want the book to be. The most common sizes are 5" x 8", 5.5" x 8.5" and 6" x 9". A variety of other sizes are available, but these are the most common. For most clients, I recommend that they use the 5" x 8" size (unless their book is very long). It seems silly, but book buyers value the thickness of a book. A smaller page size will mean a higher page count and a thicker, more attractive book.

The only exception to that rule is a poetry book. Poetry books typically put a lot more emphasis on the cover art, and don't usually have a lot of pages anyway. A larger front cover provides more room for the artwork to shine.

The designer will take the information you've provided and your digital text files (your manuscript as a word processor document), and in a couple of weeks return a book as a PDF.

In some cases, the designer may also offer a proofreading service, but in most cases, they'll provide the PDF to you and give you an opportunity to proof the book. We'll talk more about proofreading in the chapter titled "Proofreading," but once it's complete you'll provide a printed copy of the book with notes on it back to the designer, who will make the final changes.

When those changes are complete, the designer will provide a PDF of the book. Upon request, most designers will also provide an .epub (e-book file) and a .mobi (Amazon.com Kindle book file). Make sure the designer knows you want these things before you begin.

Hiring a Designer

Craigslist is always an option, but you can likely find an established business (or professional freelancer) who can take care of this for you. Simply search for a "book designer" near you on Google. Lots of regional magazines outsource their design to local designers, so even medium-sized cities should have a few options to choose from.

Always ask for examples of the designer's work, and agree upon a price and time table up front. If you'd like an e-book file too, the designer needs to know that right away.

Ask the designer about proofing the book, and how much it costs to make changes. Typically, at least one round of simple revisions is included, but be sure to ask. If you want to make more changes in six months or a year, how much will it cost then? Will the designer provide source files so that someone else can make changes down the road, or will you have to come back to them?

Common Pitfalls

1. *Trust your designer.* You're a book author, not a book designer. The biggest mistake I see self-publishers make is to provide their designer with bad instruc-

tions, and then to reject the designer's feedback and suggestions. At Columbus Publishing Lab, I always tell my staff designers that we should do our best to give good advice, but at the end of the day, the customer is the boss. If you suggest something and the designer says "I'm not sure that's a good idea, because…" that's a nice way of telling you that it's a really bad idea. Listen to your designer. They've spent a lot of time learning what makes books easy to read, and learning what the conventions of each genre are, let them do their job. If you insist, a good designer will follow your instructions, and it will be your book that turns out poorly, and it will be your fault.

2. *Don't use weird fonts.* Don't use weird fonts, ever. I've seen self-published horror books in a typeface that looks like it's dripping blood. Bad idea! Even if it looks neat for ten seconds, will your readers like it after they spend five hours with your book? Listen to your designer's advice, and stick with standard, easily-readable fonts, at least for your main text.

3. *Don't ask for big changes in the text.* When you give the text to the designer, it's set in stone. All you'll be doing after that is making minor changes—like typos. When you get the book back and have a chance to proofread it, don't make any big changes. The

designer doesn't care if you never really liked the paragraph on page twenty-seven and want to rewrite it, this is not the time. When you give the files to the designer to start his work, you're done, *finito*, your opportunity to make changes is gone. Forever. If you do absolutely need to make changes, don't beat the designer up if there's an extra fee to do that.

4. *Ask for an e-book file up front.* For many designers, it won't matter that much, it's the same program to design a print book or an e-book, it just adds a few minutes at the end to export it a different way. But that's not always true, especially if you have a complex design. So make sure to let the designer know up front (before they even quote the project) that you also want e-book files. It will likely only cost a little bit more if you ask up front, but if you ask at the end, prepare to be shocked by the price!

5. *Specify who's printing the book, and any special requirements.* It's helpful to have an idea of who will be printing the book at this point, as different printers have different requirements as far as margins, minimum font sizes, etc. Your designer should know or be able to find the specific requirements for your printer, but let them know who you may be using up front. If you switch printers after the design process, you may have to ask your designer to make some

changes to the design. Expect to pay an extra fee.

The Do-It-Yourself Way

This step is absolutely possible, but very difficult to do yourself. I've personally talked to so many self-publishers who say that the one thing they wish they would have hired out but didn't was the interior design.

It's not that it's difficult or the tools aren't available, but there are a lot of requirements that are easy to miss and difficult to understand. Most printers want to work with designers, not consumers, so they're not very accommodating or helpful when you do run into problems with their specifications.

Within the book design itself, without some experience and knowledge, the process can be extremely difficult. The one word self-publishers use over and over again to describe trying to design the interior of their book is "frustrating." If this is your first time, you'll likely repeat the process a dozen times and spend literally hundreds of hours doing it.

All of that said, you can do this step yourself. You can lay out your book in Microsoft Word (with page breaks, the right page size, page numbers, etc.) and then upload that to a service like CreateSpace that will process it for their printers. On the e-book side of things, once you have it laid out there are services like BookBaby or Smashwords that will convert your book into the correct e-book formats.

The disadvantage, in addition to the hundreds of frustrating hours, is that you'll be limited to printers willing to help you (like CreateSpace or Lulu), and as a result, you're going to get significantly fewer options for the printing, and much worse rates for the printing and distribution.

Also, keep in mind that these free processes are run by machines, that's why they can do it for free. There's little or no oversight by humans (let alone designers), so any formatting or layout errors will likely show up in the first print run.

The most common mistake that non-designers make is to mix up the minimum required margins, which is the white space between the edge of your text and the edge of your page. Some printers have very specific requirements for these margins, others let you do whatever you want. Make sure you know how to set that up before you begin.

The second most common mistake is to fail to set up the page size. You can change the size of the page to match what you'd like to be printed. I once had a guy ask me what size font to use so that when the page was shrunk down to book size, it would look right. He was designing his book in Microsoft Word. Make sure that the page size matches what the book will be.

The detailed instructions are beyond the scope of this handbook, but there are lots of resources available online for someone who wants to design the interior of their own book. If you're prepared to invest the time, the interior design can be accomplished with moderate results with software you likely already own, like Microsoft Word.

The Parts of a Book

You'll need to know the parts of your book, whether you decide to design the interior yourself or hire a designer. For fiction books, here are a few pages you'll need to know:

Half Title ("Bastard Title") Page - This is the first page of the book that typically only lists the title of the book or the publisher's name on the upper half of the page.

Foreword/Introduction - Most fiction books do not have a foreword or an introduction, but you can. If you're publishing a book of short stories, a foreword is more common.

Acknowledgments - For a fiction book, the acknowledgments can be placed at the front or the back. Keep this short. In a few sentences, and no more than a few paragraphs, thank the people who have played a real role in the creation of your book. Don't forget the nice editors who have helped. Note that this section is spelled "Acknowledgments," not "acknowledgements," there's no e after the g.

Dedication - The dedication page is optional.

Praise or Previously Published Work - There is a blank page between the half title and the regular title page. This is a great place to either put a list of other books published by the author, or some quotes from critics and other authors praising your book.

Table of Contents - Most fiction books do not contain a table of contents.

Blank Pages - Some elements (like the title page) must be on the right side of the book. For other elements, it's up to you whether it's OK for them to start on the left side, or whether you should insert a blank page to start the section on the right side. You can also let your designer make this decision.

Here is the order of the elements:

- Half Title (opening page, right side)
- Praise Quotes or Previously Published Work (or a blank page)
- Title Page (right side)
- Copyright Page (sometimes called Colophon)
- Table of Contents (if desired)
- Foreword/Introduction

- Acknowledgments (if you'd like it in the front)
- Dedication (this can be placed anywhere to fill a blank page)
- Book Content (all chapters)
- Acknowledgments (if you'd like it in the back)
- About the Author

If you hire a designer, you should have all of the parts that you'd like (including the "Acknowledgments" and "About the Author") ready before you begin.

The Columbus Publishing Lab Way

At Columbus Publishing Lab, we want to make things easy, and we want you to have confidence in our expertise.

Interior design is included in all of our packages. It can also be quoted independently if you're not using our services for the complete publication process.

Our qualified designers will take a careful look at the materials you're providing, as well as any examples you'd like us to follow, and return an elegant book that matches your genre and is print-ready for your specified printer.

With one of our packages, you can rest assured that the project will flow smoothly from copy editing to the interior design, and through the proofreading and corrections process.

The interior design will be affordable, hassle-free and your book will look great. No one will believe that you self-published.

The Take Away

You can do the interior design yourself. Lots of people do. It will be frustrating, it will take ten times as long as you expect and you may need to replace a few smashed keyboards, but you can do it yourself using a program you already own, like Microsoft Word, with adequate results.

If you decide to hire it out, you'll be glad that you did. You don't have to be rich to know that paying $300 to save 200 hours of frustrating tinkering is a hell of a deal. And a book designed in Microsoft Word compared side-by-side to a professionally produced book will be noticeably inferior.

Step Four
Proofreading

Your book is looking good and it's been edited. Now we can get that thing to the printer, right?

Not quite yet. But almost.

Proofreading is the last step before your book goes to the printer. This is your final opportunity to catch any last-minute mistakes or problems with the layout that may have arisen during the interior design process.

This is not an opportunity to fix that sentence that's always bothered you on page ninety-six, and this is not an opportunity to remove chapter four, which never really worked anyway. You're only looking for typos and obvious errors.

In the Publishing Industry

Proofreading is important. Some readers won't notice grammatical errors, but they will notice typos and they will notice if the last page of a chapter only has one word on it.

The proofreader's job is different from the copy editor's job. While the copy editor's job is to conform your work to a style guide (with all of those rules), the proofreader's job is simply to look for obvious errors and inconsistencies. The proofreader doesn't care whether your style guide dictates that "okay" should be spelled out, rather than written as "OK." All the proofreader cares about is that it's "okay" on page twenty-three, but "OK" on page ninety-one.

The proofreader's job is also broader than the copy editor's job. The proofreader is not just looking for typos and missed grammatical errors, they're also checking that the layout is the same on every page, that the page numbers are correct and that the headers are spelled correctly. The proofreader is checking things that the copy editor never had, like the title page and the copyright page.

Proofreading is not just reading and looking for mistakes, it's a specialized skill that takes some talent and a lot of practice. Most humans would never notice that "Jeep" is capitalized in chapter one, but not capitalized in chapter seven. Proofreaders are a rare bunch who can keep track of everything at the same time and somehow compare every page of the book to every other page of the book.

Why Is Proofreading Important?
You already hired an editor, you should be good to go,

right? Sorry, but no. Here are three reasons why proofreading is important.

1. *Even good copy editors miss stuff.* Copy editors are only human after all. A professional copy editor should fix greater than 99% of all errors. But there's still that pesky fraction of a percent left over. Your proofreader will catch any obvious errors that the copy editor missed.

2. *Sometimes errors can be introduced during the interior design (typesetting) step.* Maybe your designer was hitting CTRL+S to save your design, and mistakenly dropped an extra *s* into the middle of a paragraph. Or perhaps chapter three ends with one word on the last page, and the designer just didn't notice. Or maybe the page numbers are off, or the headers contain a misspelling on half of the pages. Maybe the page number is missing on the first page of chapter four. A proofreader will look for all of these things and catch them.

3. *This is your last chance to correct any mistakes before you order a bunch of books.* You've already spent a lot of time and money putting together a great book, it's worth it to spend another week and a little bit more money to make sure that everything is ready to go.

I've never sent a book to a proofreader (even books put together by the best copy editors and designers) and not gotten a list of changes back. Never once.

What Should I Expect
Your proofreader will typically return a printed manuscript to you with notes marked directly on the page. Sometimes, they'll ask you to print the manuscript on regular paper and give it to them, or sometimes they'll print it themselves.

Proofreading doesn't take long, but like all qualified professionals, good proofreaders may have a backlog of work. I've had manuscripts turned around in as little as three days, but other times it takes up to two weeks.

Proofreading is one of the least expensive tasks you'll undertake for your book. You should expect to pay $100 to $300 for a professional proofreader. Your proofreader may ask for a sample before providing an estimate.

Hiring a Proofreader
The fact is that most proofreaders I've worked with do not proofread as a full-time job. That would be an exhausting profession. If you can find a full-time professional proofreader, that's going to be a great fit, but don't be afraid to accept a moonlighter on this one.

But that also means you need to watch out for posers and unqualified applicants. Anybody can claim to be an amazing proofreader, there's no degree or certification for it after all. Make sure to ask for samples, and make sure that your applicant was the only proofreader for the samples they've provided. I've had proofreaders tell me how qualified they are and list organizations and projects they've worked with, but they can't provide a single sample that they've proofread alone. No samples, no job (or at least get a rock bottom price).

Know what you're prepared to pay and stick to it. With full-time proofreaders, you might have a little less leverage, but moonlighters are making *extra* money, so they're in a position to be more flexible. Always have a fair price in mind (the proofreader will probably spend six to eight hours with your book, and they deserve a generous wage), but don't feel like you need to accept every quote without haggling.

Craigslist is a great way to find a proofreader. Simply post your job in the "Gigs" section with as much information as possible. In Columbus, Ohio, you'll receive 10+ responses within twenty-four hours from a variety of different professionals offering a spectrum of rates. Always be suspicious of a quote that undercuts the others by too much.

The Buck Has to Stop Eventually
After hiring a proofreader, I always do a final check of the manuscript myself. Remember, if it's not broke, don't fix it. But make a last check for anything the proofreader might have missed. Even if you're hiring the best, you'll probably find a few things.

If the copy editor catches 99.1% of the errors, and the proofreader catches 99.1% of the remaining errors, there's still a tiny fraction of a percent remaining. Depending on how many errors you started with, there may still be a few.

But don't beat yourself up about it, even books produced by the biggest traditional publishers typically still have an error or two. The next time you read a mass market paperback, keep an eye out for errors—you'll probably find one.

In any case, it's your book. You're the author, the producer and you'll be the marketer. At the end of the day you are the person that the public will hold accountable for the quality of your book. Make it count.

The Do-It-Yourself Way

With the help of a friend, you can proofread your book yourself. Just like copy editing, we're often blind to our own mistakes, so I recommend that you have another set of eyes on it. In fact, the more eyes the better.

Whenever you have a friend help, always brief him on what you expect him to look for. Here's all of the things that should be checked on every page:

- Typos
- Grammatical errors
- Paragraph indentations are all the same
- Eliminate extra spaces between sentences

- Layout mistakes
- Page numbers are correct
- Header and footer are correct
- Chapter titles are correct and punctuated the same
- The title page is correct
- Copyright page is correct
- Page numbers on table of contents are correct (if applicable)

When he's done, take it to another friend and have her go through it again.

The Columbus Publishing Lab Way

We believe that proofreading is very important. That's why it's included in every one of our packages that includes copy editing. We don't think it's a job that a person can effectively do for forty hours per week (it takes too much concentration), so we have a network of part-time proofreaders that we use.

Whether you get proofreading as part of a package or purchase it *a la carte*, the cost is very affordable. When clients see what comes back, they're always happy that they hired a proofreader. Some of those mistakes would have been embarrassing!

Rinse and Repeat

Now that the proofreading is done, you can take the

changes back to your designer. It should be a quick fix, and then they'll provide the final PDF file for your printer, as well as any e-book files that you've requested.

The Take Away

Proofread your book. It's not that expensive, and you will catch errors. It's best to hire someone, but friends can do it if you're short on cash. Remember, the buck stops with you—even though you'll miss some of your own mistakes, do the last check yourself.

Step Five
Cover Design

Despite what your mother told you, these days it's more important than ever to judge a book by its cover. With the expanding publishing marketplace, where anybody can slap a "book" together with almost no investment and no quality standard, there has to be a way to tell the good from the bad.

Chances are that if someone puts together a professional cover, they've also invested the time and money into producing the rest of their book at a professional level.

In the Publishing Industry

Book covers are extremely important to the traditional book publishing industry. The book cover defines the target audience.

Most books are hybrid-genre books. This book is a science fiction crime thriller, that book is a paranormal mystery romance. Very few books are strictly "Science Fiction" or only a "Mystery." With the book cover, the publisher will solidify the book into one specific genre. Depending on the publisher's market research and the book's strengths, they'll pick one genre to really push the book.

Whether the science fiction crime thriller has a flying car or a loaded gun on the cover will dramatically affect who's interested in buying the book. Whether the paranormal mystery romance book has a half-naked hunk or a werewolf howling at the moon on the front will have a huge impact on who reads the book and what kind of reviews they leave.

Book covers don't just attract readers. They're also a solicitation to the reader's friends. I wouldn't be caught dead reading a book with a half-naked hunk on the cover. But I would sit at the bus stop and read a book with a werewolf on the front. For other readers the opposite is true. Who wants to be noticed reading the book will affect the way that the book spreads through the public.

In the traditional publishing industry, a good cover will turn away as many readers as it attracts. But nonetheless, publishers will opt for a bold choice, instead of a run-of-the-mill generic cover. Go big or go home.

If you look through a bookstore, you'll notice that the better known the author is, the more boring the cover is. This is because at some point the author's name alone will attract readers, so publishers don't need to make a bold choice that may turn some readers away. But for authors who need to attract new readers, a decisive, genre-specific cover is the way to go.

What You Should Expect

The first question to ask yourself is, what one person do you want to read your book? This is a tough question. Most authors say, "Well, I want everyone to read my book." Too bad. For this exercise, you must choose one specific type of reader. How old are they? What job do they have? How were they educated? What are their hobbies?

Armed with that answer, you can decide what kind of cover will attract that specific buyer. I know you want everyone to buy your book, and hopefully they will. But if you want to attract new readers, you must seek a specific person.

Once you have that information, let your cover designer do his job. Choose a designer who has done work similar to what you're looking for. But once you select him, provide all of your ideas and information and then step back, and let him do what he does best.

If you can't do that, then be prepared to tell your designer EXACTLY what you want and provide specific examples of similar elements from other designs. The worst case scenario with the highest cost and poorest results is to have your designer chasing a vague idea that you have. The "I'll know it when I see it" approach will generally pull the designer away from his strengths, and result in a lot of unused drafts (which means a greater cost for you).

You will need to provide some technical information to your designer. You can begin the cover design process before the proofreading is complete. However, the cover designer will need to know your book's spine height. The spine height is the thickness of the book, which is determined by the number of pages and the type of paper used. Typically, your interior designer will tell you how many pages the book will be, and you'll take this information to your chosen printer, who can give you the dimensions of the book cover.

You'll also need to know the height and width of the book, but you should have made that decision before the interior designer began.

At the end of the day, the cover designer will typically provide you with a PDF of your book cover.

How you get to the end product varies from designer to designer. Some designers will provide a single price up front which includes unlimited revisions, others will charge you per draft. Some designers will charge you by the hour (so you pay less for simple revisions and more for big revisions). These are all valid approaches, just make sure you know what you're getting before you begin, and when additional charges will be incurred.

Hiring a Cover Designer

A typical book cover design will cost between $200 and $1,000. The biggest factor is the complexity of the design. If you want a custom oil painting for the cover, that's going to cost a lot. If you have a photo, and you just want text laid over the top of it, you'll get a very low price.

The other factor is experience. Any cover designer should be able to show you examples of her work (even if it's an art school student, she should have something). When you look at the provided examples, you're looking for two things: professionalism and style. Does the artist have the skill to produce a professional-caliber cover design? Does the artist's style and medium match what you're looking for?

Don't hire an artist who has photo-based covers to do a watercolor painting for your cover. Don't hire a watercolor painter to do a digital design. It may seem obvious, but the most common mistake is to assume that just because a person is "artistic" she can provide any type of art. Make sure that what you're looking for aligns with the artist's strengths (based on her samples, not on what she says), and don't be afraid to shop around.

You can hire a moonlighter (someone who works a different type of day job) for your cover design, as long as they can provide samples of past work. It may be a stereotype, but artists can be unreliable (and the cover artist is a different animal than the interior designer), so make sure to have a verified way to contact the artist, and make sure that your time table is set in stone. Check in with your artist once a week until it's done, but not every day. And if a deadline passes and it's not done (especially if the artist is unreachable), move on.

A full-time artist will typically ask for 50% up front, with the other half due upon completion. Some artists will break the payment into three parts, with a third due up front, a third due when the first draft is complete and approved, and the final payment due when the digital file is delivered. This is fine.

However, if you hire a moonlighter, offer 10% up front and stick to it. As soon as it's done, promptly pay your bill.

The Do-It-Yourself Way

You can design your cover yourself. Most of the time it will be obvious that it was done by an amateur, but you can do it with decent results. Services like CreateSpace provide some user-friendly tools for designing a cover if you use their publishing service, and there are also plenty of free photo editing programs that will do the trick.

Before you begin, make sure you know the cover dimensions and resolution that your printer requires. Depending on your printer, they may or may not be helpful with this. You'll need to know the total size of the cover (including any "bleed," which is the amount of overhang on the edges that will be cut off), and the size of the spine in the middle.

Remember that the cover is one big piece of paper that wraps around the pages. That means that the front of the cover will be on the right side, and the back of the book will be on the left side.

Don't use copyright images. I once had a kind older gentleman explain to me that when you create a book, you can, "Just go to Google, type in anything you want, right click the image and download it. Then use it for your cover." Please don't do that. You may only use photos and images that you have the rights to use. If you find it on the Internet and it doesn't say something like "You may use this photo for free," you should assume that it's off-limits.

You can find "Creative Commons" files that are licensed to the public to use for free. A great resource for free photos is MorgueFile.com. But even Creative Commons licenses have restrictions, so make sure to read carefully and please follow the guidelines that the creator requested.

Just remember, you may NOT legally use most of the images that you find on the Internet. Just don't do it.

If you use a photo for your cover, make sure that the resolution is high enough. Most computer screens display at a resolution of 72 dots per inch. But most book covers are printed at 300 (or higher) dots per inch. You don't have to be a graphics expert to know that 300 is a lot more than 72. That means that a photo that looks great on your computer screen might look pixelated and crummy when printed on a book cover.

Writers are not typically great book cover designers. And there are some technical parameters (and some vocabulary) that can be hard to master unless you're really committed to spending a lot of time on it. But you can design your own cover, just make sure that you have the legal right to use all of the imagery.

What to Include on the Cover
There are a few elements that your book cover must in-

clude, the rest is up to you. Always include the title of the book and the author's name on the front of the book. If your book has a subtitle, you can include that too.

On the back of the book, you must have a barcode, and it's a good idea to include the name and/or logo of the publisher or imprint that will be producing the book (or your own name).

The back of the book can also include your choice of critical praise for the book, a description or tease for the book, or a very short author bio.

The spine of the book should include the title of the book (typically the subtitle is not included here), and the author's last name. Sometimes the publisher's icon/logo will also be at the bottom of the spine.

The Columbus Publishing Lab Way

At Columbus Publishing Lab, we keep things simple. Cover design is included in most of our packages.

We have two cover design prices.

Photo-based covers are inexpensive, and we call these "Standard Covers." Clients either provide a photo that they would like used, or they choose from a photo in our extensive library that we've purchased the legal right to use.

We also maintain an extensive network of skilled artists for covers with custom artwork, which we call "Premium Covers." From oil paintings to watercolors, to custom photography and digital design, we have experienced artists who can complete the artwork quickly and at an affordable cost. Premium book covers are quoted on a case-by-case basis, except for clients who select "The Catalyst," a self-publishing package that includes a premium cover.

Whether clients choose the standard or premium cover design service, a marketing consultant will review the front and back cover text that the client has selected, and the Laboratory Assistant (the client's personal assistant and book coach) will work with the client to put together a highly effective book cover.

The Take Away

The book cover is another job that you can successfully do yourself. If you're committed to learning, and doing it several times until it's right, you can put together a decent cover.

However, don't believe for a second that it's "the words that count." Your cover design is critical to the book, and it will have a huge impact on your total sales.

If you design the cover yourself, make sure that you're targeting a specific reader, and make sure that you can legally use the imagery that you've chosen.

Cover design can be expensive, especially if you'd like custom drawings or paintings. But if you'd like to use a professional, there are affordable cover designs that will do the trick and make your book look like a first-class operation.

E-Book Only Production

If you'd like to only produce an e-book, your process will still be much the same.

Editing for an E-book
You'll still need to get developmental editing and copy editing for an e-book, and it will cost the same amount. The standard of quality isn't relaxed in any way because the book is digital. Nothing will change from the print book process.

Interior Design
If you only want an e-book, the interior design process can be simplified. E-books have fewer constraints than what a printer typically requires, so it should be a little cheaper and quicker. Some services will call this "e-book conversion," and you can usually find a deal for about $100.

Some services, like CreateSpace or Smashwords, will offer a free conversion process. Just make sure you know what you're getting, as you'll likely also be obligated to use their distribution or other services if you use their conversion process. You may also permanently give up the rights to distribute your book elsewhere. Read the fine print.

Cover Design

The cover design is quicker and easier too. E-books only need the front half of the cover, and the required resolution is much lower than what's required for a print book. This will reduce the cost of the cover design significantly. You can likely find a pretty good designer who will do a professional-quality e-book cover for $100 to $300.

You May Not Save That Much

Even if you're only intending to produce an e-book, it can be a good idea to complete the full cover design and interior design process. Even if you don't use it right away, it may not cost that much more to complete the full print process, and then at least you'll have the files if you decide that you need them later.

You're really only saving on the design aspect of the project. So what may cost you a total of $700 for the interior and cover design of a print book will only cost $300 for an e-book. But if you only produce an e-book, you'll have to start over and pay the full $700 again if you decide to print a book in the future. At that time, you'll kick yourself for being so shortsighted and not just finding a way to make the extra $400 happen.

Ask your designer what the price difference will be for an e-book only compared to the full print book and e-book. It may be worth shelling out a little more up front.

Printing Your Book

Your book is now complete. You've edited your manuscript and the interior of the book has been designed. You proofread the book, made a few small changes and now the text is in good shape. You have a PDF of the interior of your book.

You also came by a cover design, and you have a PDF of the properly sized cover at a high enough resolution for your printer.

Nice work! You're now ready to take your book to the printer.

There are three types of book printing that concern us. "Print-on-Demand," "Short-Run Printing" and "Offset Printing."

Offset Printing

Offset printing is generally used for print-runs of 1,000

books or more. This is the cheapest type of printing and generally comes with substantial discounts.

Most self-publishers don't print this many books at one time. Remember that anything you print you have to store or ship, both of which are expensive.

Short-Run Printing

Short-run printing is for lower quantities of books. Generally, the more books you order, the greater of a per-book discount you'll receive.

Most self-publishers choose to print a small number of books to keep on hand, so that they can give some away to reviewers, and sell them to friends, family or at events. A box or two of books can be shoved under a bed or into a closet somewhere.

Print-On-Demand

Print-on-demand books are printed when they're ordered. This is the best option for the day-to-day operations for most self-publishers. You don't have to commit any cash, and you don't have to fill your spare bedroom with boxes of books.

Columbus Publishing Lab uses a print-on-demand service to fulfill orders to Amazon and other retailers. So when a customer orders your book off of Amazon.com, Amazon then orders the book from Columbus Publishing Lab, who has a book printed and shipped. With digital printing, this process happens extremely quickly. The customer never knows the difference (the book will be delivered to Amazon the same day, just like if they plucked it from their warehouse), and Amazon saves a lot of money on warehousing.

Amazon receives the money from the customer. They keep some of it and pay the rest to Columbus Publishing Lab. We deduct the cost of the printing and give you the rest. You never had to touch a book or worry about a thing, and you get a check!

Of course, you do receive a bit less than if you printed 1,000 books and shipped them out yourself. But the convenience is well worth the cost. You'll also save significant time and frustration with the distribution process, which will be addressed in the next chapter.

The Best Strategy

The best strategy for self-publishers is to combine short-run and print-on-demand printing. When you create your book, you'll want to order a small supply. You can give books to family and friends, sell them at local author events and send free books to reviewers. You also may sell a few books through your personal website that you'll want to ship out yourself.

But…let print-on-demand work its magic. Packing and shipping books is a pain in the butt, and you have to store them somewhere. Print-on-demand is an affordable way to extend your reach to new retailers, and it comes with little up-front cost to you.

Print-on-demand used to carry a stigma. But it's no longer something for fly-by-night operations. Even the largest traditional publishers are using print-on-demand technology to make their businesses more efficient and to extend their reach.

The last thing you want is to start receiving orders for your book and to spend every afternoon waiting in line at the post office to ship one or two books. You've got better things to do. You're a writer who happens to be marketing a book after all, not a pack-and-ship clerk.

One of the most common mistakes that self-publishers make post-production is to over-order their books. Take full advantage of digital technology, and order books when you need them. Granted, you'll get a discount for ordering more books, but the savings won't compensate for turning your living room into a warehouse. It's better to print fewer books and to devote the capital you have left over to marketing your book.

Book Distribution

You've got a first-class book. It's been edited, designed and even printed. Now you can just walk into Barnes & Noble, tell them about your book and they'll buy it from you, right? Sorry, not so fast.

The book industry has a rigid system of distribution.

How Distribution Works

With thousands of publishers in America, bookstores don't want to order a few copies from each one. They don't want to place thousands of tiny orders with a thousand different companies, and then write a thousand checks for a few dollars each. Instead, they only order from distributors.

A distributor, like Ingram, collects titles from lots of publishers, big and small, and presents them all to the bookstore. The bookstore picks out everything it wants to carry on its shelves, places one giant order from the distributor, and then writes one big check. The distributor then delivers one big truckload of books.

The distributor handles the accounting and management of all of the little publishers, and makes sure that everyone gets paid. When this system was created it was a genius move to compartmentalize the warehousing and fulfillment process, and to make the book ordering process more efficient.

A retailer like Barnes & Noble can work with several distributors, rather than thousands of tiny publishers. This cuts down on their administrative costs and streamlines their business.

Distributors have historically acted as a gatekeeper as well. They won't pick up any piece of junk that every tiny publisher with a Xerox machine puts out. The distributor only wants to carry books that are likely to sell. They have limited warehouse space, after all, and they need to maintain their reputation with the booksellers.

But that's all changing, thanks to digital technology.

Distribution for You

For a relatively small fee, practically anyone can now pay to be added to a distributor's catalog. Once you're added, your book will instantaneously be available to that distributor's clients. The distributor's function as the gatekeeper is growing obsolete. If you've got the cash, you're in.

This is great news for you. In the past, you would have worked hard to get your book accepted by a distributor, now you just shell out a few bucks and the job is done.

But since the distributor is no longer the gatekeeper, you have a new job.

Your New Job

Just because your book is available to the big bookstores through a distributor doesn't mean that they'll carry it on their shelves. It will be available for special order, like if someone walks up to the counter and says, "Can you get me a copy of Joe Author's *The Long, Hard Road*?" But shelf space is valuable and there are millions of titles available, so don't expect to walk into your nearest Barnes & Noble and see your book on the "New Arrivals" table.

Now that you're in a distributor's catalog, your job is to convince bookstores everywhere to carry your book. If you have a distributor and the bookstore agrees to carry it, it's at their fingertips. They can order it on the same order form with all of their other books.

But it can be a tough sell.

The process will be different at every brick and mortar retailer. Smaller stores will have a manager (or maybe even the owner) whose job is to order books. You just need to get in a room with that person and ask them to order your book. If the book looks good, the price is right, the book is returnable (more on this in a minute), and you're a nice person, the buyer at a local, independent bookstore will probably order your book.

It won't be the same story at the chain stores.

Bigger stores will have an extensive application process. Barnes & Noble, for instance, has a "Small Press" process, by which you fill out a formal application and present documents that demonstrate your book's assets and your commitment to marketing the book. The process will take many weeks and, frankly, the odds of success aren't that high. There are millions of books available to a big store like that, and they just don't have shelf space for all of them. If you pursue that process, make sure that you follow all of the instructions, and you might just get lucky.

The good news is that once you're in with a reputable distributor, your book will be available from almost all online book retailers, like Amazon.com and BarnesandNoble.com. Through the beauty of on-demand printing, there's no risk for an online retailer, so they'll carry everything. When a customer orders your book, the retailer will order a single copy from your distributor. Your distributor will have the book printed the same day and fulfill the order to the customer. It's a wonderful thing! You get a check, and you didn't even know it was happening!

Practically Speaking

Distributors set their own rules. So how all of this actually plays out depends on which distributor you use. Some distributors will warehouse your books for you, others will work with an on-demand printer on your behalf. You'll need to talk to some potential distributors to find out how things might work for you.

At Columbus Publishing Lab, distribution is included in all of our self-publishing packages. We provide your digital files to an on-demand printer. When a book is ordered, we print and fulfill it. We take a small charge for the distribution and pay for the printing, and the rest of the money is yours to keep. It's simple and hassle-free, that way you can concentrate on more important things, like marketing your book and writing the sequel.

If You Print Your Own Books

It's a common rookie mistake to rush out and find a printer near you, and to order 1,000 books at a great price break. The first-time self-publisher typically surveys the grand stack of boxes of books they've just received and then says, "Now how do I get Amazon.com to carry my books?"

Amazon has a program for you called "Amazon Advantage." You can find it at advantage.amazon.com. They'll order your book from you, stock it in their warehouse and ship it out to customers when they order. It's a consignment program, so you get paid when they sell the book.

The Advantage program requires a 55% discount off of the list price. You'll also need to ship the books to the Amazon warehouse at your expense. There's also an annual fee of about $30 to be enrolled in the program.

The bad news is that Amazon doesn't want to waste warehouse space on a bunch of self-published books that probably won't sell. So they're going to order one or two books from you. When they receive the book, it'll show up as "In-stock" on their website. They'll wait until the book sells, it will show up as "Out of Stock" and then they'll order one more book from you. When it arrives at their warehouse, they'll update their website. It gets worse.

If you price your book at $14.95, Amazon will pay you about $6.73 per book that they sell. That's not bad, but remember that you have to ship the book to them as well. That's going to cost you about $2.50 per book by media mail (they're only going to order one book at a time, maybe two). So your payout is now down to $4.23 per book. You're probably already busted, but if you're still profitable don't forget that you paid for the envelope, for the tape, you're going to wait in line at the post office for twenty minutes to send every book, and, oh yeah, there's that $30 annual fee.

Very few self-published authors can turn a profit this way. But many choose to take a loss, simply to have their book listed and sold on Amazon.com.

Your other option is to pursue a warehousing distributor. Near Columbus, Ohio there's a distributor called Atlas Books (Ashland, Ohio). In order to be distributed by their company, you need to lease space in their warehouse, and then they'll handle the pack-and-ship for you. This is legitimate, you'll be able to set your own prices and discounts, just like through a print-on-demand distributor, and your book will be available to all of the retailers who use the distributor you've contracted.

However, there's a lot of overhead. At Atlas Books, there's a $500 account setup fee, and you'll have to pay monthly fees to keep your books in the warehouse (you generally pay by the cubic foot). You'll also pay for every shipment they send out. Not to mention, all of your inventory is now tied up in a warehouse somewhere. Due to the high overhead and startup costs, this option is generally only viable for larger publishing operations.

You can make either of these options work, especially if you know what you intend to do before you begin. You can price your books a little higher and make Amazon Advantage work, or you can set aside some startup cash to get established with a warehousing distributor.

But at the end of the day, unless you're moving high volume, that 30% you saved by printing 1,000 books up front will always be lost in the overhead and fees associated with these distribution methods.

If you've printed a lot of books before thinking about distribution, the best option is usually to keep the books you've printed for direct sales through your website, events, reviewers, etc., but to set up your distribution to major retailers through a print-on-demand service.

I recently consulted with a gentleman in exactly this situation. He had printed 500 copies of his 398-page book. The printer handled the book layout and printing for about $6 per book, and he had set his list price at $14.95 per book. He received the book and it looked great. Then he started investigating how to get it on Amazon.com and on the shelf at Barnes & Noble. He thought if he could bring in $10 per book, he could break even at 300 books.

He was at his wit's end. He'd spent hours on the phone with Amazon, getting passed from one department to the other. Nobody seemed to be able to even point him towards Amazon Advantage.

He contacted me and we sat down and went through his options. We talked about Amazon Advantage, but at the end of the day, he'd lose more than $1.75 per book sold there. He couldn't sell books at a loss.

We talked about a warehousing distributor, but he'd already invested $3,000, he didn't want to drop $500+ more and get a bill every month.

Eventually, we decided that he would keep his inventory for direct sales through his website, as well as send a lot more books to reviewers. But we would use a print-on-demand distributor to get the book out to Amazon.com and other retailers. He would set his discount at 20%, and focus on driving sales through online retailers. The total cost to set this up, including e-book distribution to the four largest e-book markets as well, was only $299.

After that cost, he's home free. Every book that sells, he gets a check for about $5. That's money in the bank, with virtually no overhead.

It's unfortunate that we couldn't put the $3,000 worth of books that he already purchased to good use, but at the end of the day it made a lot more sense to cut his losses and proceed down a more profitable route.

Within a week, his book was listed on Amazon.com and BarnesandNoble.com.

The sweet spot in the center is that he had a lot of extra books to send out to reviewers, and that will be a great boost for his project.

The long and short is that unless you have a lot of capital to devote to your project, print-on-demand distribution is usually the way to go. Even if you make a mistake and print a bunch of books up front, you'll likely be better served to make use of your books as best you can, but to use a print-on-demand distributor to get your books out to retailers.

Pricing Your Book

You want to price your book cheap, right? That way more people will buy it. That's true, but if you've been paying attention, you've probably noticed that everybody and their grandmother wants a piece of the price of your book.

We'll start with a little vocabulary. The "List Price" is the price on the back of the book. It's the same thing as the MSRP (Manufacturer's Suggested Retail Price). Most bookstores will sell your book for the list price, and run any sales off of that amount.

The "Discount" indicates the price at which a bookstore can purchase your book from the distributor. Other industries use a "Wholesale" price. A book with a list price of $10 and a 40% discount will be available to bookstores for $6 per book — $10.00 x 40% = $4.00; $10.00 (your list price) - $4.00 (the discount) = $6.00 (the bookstore's wholesale price). So the bookstore will sell the book for around $10, or a little less, and anything over $6 is their profit.

"Returnable" indicates whether the bookstore can return unsold inventory.

Who Gets Paid

Self-publishing is a cash business. Everybody gets paid down the line.

The bookstore takes the discount.

The distributor takes a fee for getting the book to the bookstore.

The printer charges you to print the book.

You may have to pay to have the book shipped to the warehouse, distributor or bookstore.

You get the rest.

Oftentimes with modern print-on-demand systems, the distributor and the printer's charges will be lumped together as a single amount.

For our $10 book in the example above, the bookstore gets 40% off, which leaves you with $6. Together, the printer and the distributor take $4.25 for printing the book and getting it to the bookstore. Then you take home $1.75.

How to Determine Your Discount

You've got three really good options when it comes to discounts. The decision comes down to which retailers you want to carry the book.

20% - Don't go below a 20% discount. With a 20% discount, online retailers will carry your book. There's no risk to them. At 20%, there's no reason to make your book returnable. No brick-and-mortar bookstores are going to be interested in carrying your book anyway.

40% - Independent bookstores will be interested in your book, if it's returnable, at a 40% discount. Unless you're a really phenomenal salesman who is also very lucky, the larger stores will not be interested.

55% - This is considered the industry-standard discount. You're still going to have to sell your butt off and get lucky, but large chain bookstores will start to be more interested in your book.

But, you can't jack the price up to offer a bigger discount. You can't sell a $25 paperback and offer a 55% discount and expect large bookstores to be interested.

You also can't set different discounts for different types of retailers. Your distributor will offer one discount rate to all of their clients. The good news is that if you offer a larger discount, online retailers will be more inclined to mark your book down and sell it on sale.

The first question to ask is, "Am I comfortable taking the risk with returnable books?" If the answer is no (which is a good answer), then you might as well set your discount to 20%. Good job, you've got your discount. Your book will be listed with all of the major online retailers, but nowhere else.

If the answer is "Yes, I am comfortable with returnable books" the next question is, "Do I have what it takes (and am I willing to do it) to get large chain stores to carry my book?" If the answer is "No," (and if we're realistic, that's probably the right answer) then set your discount at 40%. You'll get online retailers who will be able to offer your book on sale, and you can probably convince the independent bookstore in your neighborhood to carry your book too.

If you think you've got what it takes to get chain stores to carry your book, then we move on to the 55% discount. You're not done yet, you still need to determine if it's financially viable. Can you produce a book for a low enough cost to keep the list price competitive, all the while keeping the revenue high enough to compensate for any potential returns?

Use one of these three discounts. A 45% discount is useless. It's scarcely more attractive than a 40% discount to a chain store. In reality, you're just giving the same independent bookstores that would have carried your book anyway an extra 5% gift.

Returnable Books

Brick and mortar bookstores will want to know if your book is returnable. "Returnable" books are exactly what they sound like. If the book doesn't sell, the bookstore wants to be able to return them.

This presents a big risk to the small publisher. Let's say Giant Bookstore Z likes your book, so they order 1,000 units at $10 apiece. Awesome! You have your printer whip up 1,000 books (for the cool price of $3,000) and you ship them off.

Bookstore Z splits those books among 100 retail locations, and each store sticks your book on the bottom shelf of the last row in the back. Nobody buys them.

Six months later, Bookstore Z sends back 990 books. It's not like you can have the printer un-print them. So now you're stuck with the inventory, (which you shelled out $3,000 for) which is going to rot in your basement, and you need to pay Bookstore Z $9,900 for the 990 books they returned. You can do the math later, but take it from me, you just lost $2,900.

It sounds scary and it should be. It's not that unrealistic.

But the other reality is that most bookstores won't carry books that they can't return. If you want Giant Bookstore Z to carry your book, it's got to be returnable. Some self-publishers say "Forget about Bookstore Z," and decide not to allow returns, instead focusing on online retailers. The fact is that it's unlikely that Bookstore Z was ever going to order your book in the first place (even if it's really good), so that's not a bad idea. You can avoid wasting time trying to proposition the large bookstores, and you can set a lower discount for online retailers so your take-home pay goes up. Or, with a lower discount, you can sell the book cheaper.

Many self-publishers choose to factor potential returns

into their price and take the risk. If you do accept returns and you make a big sale, don't spend the money right away. Set it aside for a while and forget about it until you have a solid sense of how your book is selling.

The Dreaded Formula

It's time to actually determine your price. You need two pieces of information. You need to know how much your printer, warehouse, distributor, shipper, etc. will charge you per book all together (fee), and you need to know how much you want to make per book (profit).

If you're just spitballing, and you know the length of your manuscript, figure 300 words per book page. So a 60,000 word manuscript will be 200 pages. Use this information to get a quick quote from your printer. Add half of this cost again to make up for shipping, distribution and whatever other costs you'll find. If the printer tells you it will be $3 per book, plan on $4.50.

If you're planning on accepting returns, I recommend that your "profit" be at least equal to what your total fee will be. Down the road, that means that if a bookstore returns half of the books they purchased, you'll still break even. Anything less is suicide.

The formula for determining your price is as follows:

Profit + Fee = (1-Discount) x Price

So if your discount is set to 40% (.40), your fee to print and distribute this book is $4 per book, and you want to make $2 per book, you can solve the equation with basic algebra:

$$\$2 + \$4 = (1-.40)X$$
$$\$6 = (.6)X$$
$$X = \$10$$

In this scenario, you should charge at least $10 per book. Anything more will result in a higher profit, and anything less will result in a lower profit.

If math isn't your strong suit, it gets easier. Most distributors will have some online tools to help you determine how much you'll make per book. You can put in your list price and the discount, and they'll tell you how much you'll make per book. You can play with the list price and the discount until you find something you're happy with.

If you allow returns, don't forget that you have to pay back the full price that the bookstore paid, not just what you made. In the above scenario you made $2 a book, but you still have to pay back $6 for every book that's returned, and you have to swallow the $4 that you paid to have the book printed.

The good news is that if you don't allow returns and you use print-on-demand, there's really no risk. If you only make fifty cents per book, that's yours to keep. That's money in the bank. That's fifty cents more than you had yesterday.

The Break Even Point

While we're on the topic of money in the bank, we might as well talk about your break even point. Remember that not all of what we've been calling "profit" is actually profit. If you've followed the instructions in this handbook and done things right, you've spent at least a little money in the production of the book. And if you want to be successful, you're also spending some money on marketing the book.

I hate to be the bearer of bad news, but you probably won't sell ten million books. What's a more realistic number? How about 500 books? Maybe 1,000?

Take the total amount you've invested in your project and divide it by the "profit" you determined you'll make per book. The result is the number of books you need to sell to break even. So if you've invested $2,000 and you've determined that your profit will be $4 per book, then you need to sell 500 books to break even.

Can you sell that many books? I think you can. But it's helpful to know how many books you need to break even before you begin. After you hit that magic sales mark, it's all gravy—you've got money in the bank.

Price High

When in doubt, price your book higher. Once you print your price on the back of the book, it's permanent. In the future, you, or retailers, can always sell the book on sale for a lower price. But if you made a mistake and your numbers aren't working out down the road, you'll never get away with selling the book for more than what it says on the back.

Most paperbacks will land in the $15 to $20 range. That may seem high, but it's OK. If you need to charge more than $20 for your paperback, you'll probably want to rethink some things.

The Business Side

You want to do things right. You know you're going to have to spend a little money. When you're working with a limited budget, the hardest part can be figuring out where to spend your precious few dollars.

How Much Do You Have to Spend?

Before beginning any new business, it's important to determine how much money you're willing to spend. Just like sitting down at a poker table, if you don't know when your wallet is "empty," you'll likely lose your shirt.

To self-publish at a professional level, $1,500 is really the bare minimum to bring to the table. That's going to give you enough money to hire editors and designers. You'll still need to hike up your britches and do a few things yourself, but overall you'll be in good shape.

It can be a tough pill to swallow, but if you're not working with at least $1,500, in most cases you'll be better off waiting. Save some money and do things right. You only get one shot to release your book. Professional publication can be done for less, but you're really going to have to make things happen, and you're going to need some luck on your side.

The truth is that the more money you bring to the table, the easier your job is. For about $5,000 you can have an absolutely top-notch book production process and a basic marketing platform established. Anything after that you can put towards marketing, which is where things really get interesting.

Whatever amount of money you've determined you have, whether it's $200 or $50,000, we now need to divide it up into the tasks that we have to accomplish.

Let's review the five steps, and determine how much money we have to spend on each one:

Developmental Editing _____
Copy Editing _____
Interior Design _____
Proofreading _____
Cover Design _____
Distribution Setup Fees _____
Initial Book Supply _____
Initial Marketing Budget _____

Let's start by crossing off anything that you intend to do yourself, or if you intend to skip that step.

Next we need to split our money into those categories. Review the minimum prices from each chapter, is there enough to go around?

If I had $1,500 to spend, I'd probably do something like this:

Developmental Editing	Workshop
Copy Editing	$200
Interior Design	$300
Proofreading	Friend
Cover Design	$300
Distribution Setup Fees	$300
Initial Book Supply	$200
Initial Marketing Budget	$200

I've got to find some bargains, and I'm going to have my friend do the proofreading. I'm going to find a writers' workshop for the developmental editing and hope for the best. I'm only going to get thirty to forty books with $200, but it's important to me that my book is listed with a good distributor so that I don't have to worry about getting my book on Amazon and everything.

I want it to look really professional, so I'm willing to spend a little more than the bare minimum on the cover design and interior design. Plus I don't have time to figure out how to do the interior design. Anything left over is going into my marketing budget.

That's a good baseline, and things can scale up from there.

To make things easier, Columbus Publishing Lab provides a list of self-publishing packages. Ranging in price from $399 to $3,999, each package includes the most important items to have professionally produced within each price range. We understand that not everyone can afford to do every step exactly right, but we're still here to help you get the most out of every dollar. All of our packages include distribution to retailers.

Don't forget to create a marketing budget. I recommend that you come up with an initial amount that you're comfortable spending (the more the better), and then set aside a percentage of every book sale to reinvest. Many authors choose to reinvest 100% of all revenue back into marketing for at least the first 500 books, then re-evaluate and begin taking a paycheck after that number of books is reached. That's a good idea if you can afford it.

When it comes to marketing, everything costs money. At the very least, you'll want to mail copies of your book to reviewers, and that's going to cost you about $3 per book just for the shipping.

You can self-publish for next to nothing. But in almost all cases, the results, both in the written word and the production of the book, will be dramatically inferior. Whether you only have a few hundred dollars, or a few thousand, commit yourself to doing things right, and play with these numbers until you find a solution that will give you the best results.

Hiring Freelancers

You've determined roughly how much money you have to spend for each job. You're looking to pay the bare minimum for some jobs, and other jobs you have a little more leverage with.

Hiring freelancers is an interesting animal. You'll meet some of the best and worst people you've ever had the pleasure to work with.

Here are some simple tips to help you make good choices when hiring a freelancer for any task, so that you can get the most out of your valuable capital.

Shop Around

It's a known fact among freelancers that most clients will hire the first person they talk to. That's great news for freelancers who answer their phone. But don't be that client!

Always interview more than one person before selecting a

freelancer. Don't rub it in their faces, but freelancers who know you're interviewing more than one person will get you a quote faster, and it will probably be a more competitive price.

You'll be surprised by the differences in the quality of service, communication and price among freelancers. Which brings me to my second tip…

Don't Always Take the Lowest Price

You get what you pay for, right? Absolutely. If you're getting multiple quotes, don't always take the lowest price. If you get four quotes and one is dramatically lower than the others, ask yourself why that person is able to provide such a low price. If you don't have an answer that makes really good sense to you, don't take that quote.

The highest price doesn't always mean the best results either. Inexperienced freelancers have a tendency to either overprice or underprice their services.

Typically, the middle of the pack knows what they're doing, are doing enough business to be familiar with the market, and are committed to growing their business and producing great results.

Know Why This Person is Freelancing

There are four common reasons why a person might be freelancing:

1. *He can't find/take a full-time job.* This isn't always bad, the economy can be tough sometimes, especially for creative services. But some things to keep in mind are, a) if they're offered a full-time job tomorrow, will they still finish your project? b) is the job market that bad, or is it just that bad for them?

2. *Students.* There are lots of students who will do a great job. The right student can be a Godsend—motivated, courteous, timely, appreciative and affordable. But students are also notorious for overstating their capabilities, not returning phone calls and not completing the job. If you're hiring a student, make sure you see examples of their work and verify that they have a history of completing jobs on time.

3. *This is extra work to make ends meet.* Moonlighters, like students, are a mixed bag. Some are motivated professionals who need a little extra money for their kid's preschool. They'll bend over backwards to make you happy. Others are working for extra beer and pizza money, or saving for vacation, and if the excrement hits the fan, you'll be their lowest priority.

4. *She's very good at what she does, and it makes sense for her to be her own boss.* This person works as a freelancer as a full-time job. It's not always a guarantee, but this person is most likely to return the best

results. She works as a freelancer because she wants to, not because she has to. If a full-time job was offered to her, she'd probably turn it down.

Number four may charge a little more. But if you can find this person, it's almost always well worth it.

Establish Hard Deadlines
Sometimes time tables are hard to predict. With creative work, sometimes it takes more time than others to come up with and implement a great idea. But when your potential freelancer says "it usually takes two to three weeks," that's your time to say, "So you'll have this complete by October 1?" Let the freelancer set the deadline, but make sure that they know that you won't accept a day later.

Don't push the freelancer to offer a quicker turnaround, unless you're willing to pay extra for it. The freelancer wants the job, and he'll likely agree to a quicker turnaround if pushed. But if you're not paying for speed with extra money, you'll probably pay for it in poorer results and worse communication. Most freelancers also know that people who are pushing for the quickest turnaround are usually the slowest to provide the materials, and it's a recipe for disaster.

If the freelancer can't make the deadline, and they let you know well in advance, allow them to push it back once.

If a deadline passes with no product (and you've provided

everything on your end in a timely manner), in firm but courteous terms let the freelancer know that he has three more days. If your product still isn't delivered, move on. Demand your deposit back, but don't expect to get it, and don't waste your time and emotional energy trying to get it back.

Sign an Agreement

It astounds me the number of people who work with a freelancer without signing a work agreement. You sign an agreement at the dry cleaner, but not to hire someone at $85 per hour?

Make sure you have an agreement in place that specifies the work to be performed, the established deadline, what happens if those deadlines aren't met, what exactly will be delivered (do you get source files or the original artwork, or just the final digital PDF?) and when payment will be due. The agreement should also specify if, and when, any additional charges can be incurred, and how you'll be billed for those.

Also verify that the agreement specifies who owns the material. Some artists will want to "license" the artwork to you for a set period of time. That's not acceptable. When you receive the product and pay the bill (not before), full ownership needs to transfer to you for all eternity.

Beyond those items, don't worry too much about the agreement. Professional freelancers will already have a form agreement with some legal jargon. Don't beat them up about the "limit of liability" clause or "death and dismemberment." If the big points are in order, just sign the thing and get on with your project.

Pay Your Bill

Always treat your freelancer like you'd like to be treated. When you sell your book, you want to get paid right away, right? Then do the same for your freelancer.

When the final product is delivered and is satisfactory, pay right away. Even if you have 30 days to pay, don't make the freelancer sweat it. Just write them a check and move on.

Never hire services before you have the money to pay. If you hire someone for a $400 project that will take four weeks, it's OK if you only have $200 now, because you're going to get paid again on the 15th, right? WRONG. You know that a thousand things can come up in the next four weeks, and if they do, will paying your freelancer be your first priority? Please, for the sake of freelancers everywhere, don't hire a freelancer until you have the full amount set aside, untouchable.

If you don't pay your bill, do not use what the freelancer has provided until the issue is resolved. A freelancer typically won't sue you because you skipped out on $200. However, if you publish a book that contains work that you do not have the right to use, the potential damages for copyright infringement skyrocket, and if you get caught, you'll owe a lot more than the original $200.

Be Kind

After you hire a freelancer, be firm, but kind. Be a client that your freelancer wants to do great work for.

Communicate accurately. When the designer asks questions, answer them right away. Return messages, respond to emails. A good freelancer has several projects at a time, quick and friendly communication will make sure that when she sits down at her desk, your project is the one she's excited to work on.

There will be times to professionally say, "This is the deadline, and according to our agreement, this is what will happen if I don't have the files in my hands." But meanness will get you nowhere. Remember, it's more important to get the files than to be right.

I know you're the boss, and you shouldn't have to cower to your hired freelancer. But think about all of the bosses you've had in your life, and think about which ones you wanted to do the best work for.

Be firm and communicate clearly, but be kind and respect your freelancer as a qualified professional, and most of the time you'll get great results.

Keep in mind that freelancers who do great work typically know other freelancers who also do great work. A fantastic interior designer that you've been nice to might just save you a lot of time and money by recommending a fantastic cover designer.

If you hire enough freelancers, you will get burned. Someone will fail to deliver, or will lie to you about their skills and capabilities. At some point, you'll probably lose a little money. It's going to happen, that's OK. When it does happen, try not to waste too much time fuming or trying to recover your time and money. The best thing to do is move on and find someone who can deliver what you're looking for.

Conclusion

In my career as a publishing consultant, I have, of course, had lots of clients who need to cut corners or want to try a different approach. There's always some new service claiming to revolutionize self-publishing, or a company that can create a book in one easy step.

I always work with the client (they're the boss), so we try to approach the issue sensibly. Yet, almost 100% of the time, at some point down the road the client will express to me that he wishes we wouldn't have cut that corner or wasted time trying that stupid thing.

At the end of the day, these five steps are rock solid. That's why publishers use them. Clients who follow them are satisfied with their books, clients who don't follow them usually wish that they had.

There are a lot of avenues available to you. You can skip all of this advice, hop on over to CreateSpace, upload your

Word document, use their "free" online tools, and in a few days you'll have a "book" in your hands.

But we both know that's not good for readers, it's not good for the publishing industry and it's not good for you. If you're going to produce a book, you owe it to yourself to do things right.

I so badly want to see more self-publishers do things right. It's the only way the industry is going to get any better.

These five steps—Developmental Editing, Copy Editing, Interior Design, Proofreading and Cover Design—will produce a professional book that your friends won't believe you self-published.

These steps will require a little money and a lot of commitment. But if you use them, you can accomplish the same things that a big publisher can, and you can produce a phenomenal piece of literature.

You have the resources at your fingertips. You can do this.

Now go, make books.

Glossary

Here are some helpful terms that you'll encounter as you produce your book:

- **Bastard Title** - Also called the half title, this is the first page of a book which only displays the title of the book or the publisher's name in the upper half of the page.

- **Bleed** - The amount of extra overhang your graphics should have so that the printer can print all the way to the edge of the paper. The printer will print the bleed beyond the edge and then cut that part off.

- **Copy Editing** - Line-by-line editing of the text to fix grammatical mistakes and to conform the text to a style guide.

- **Copyrights Page** - Sometimes called "Colophon," the copyrights page displays all of the legal information about the book, such as the copyright and ISBN numbers, and the publisher's contact information.

- **Cover Design** - The process of designing the cover for your book.

- **Deposit** - The amount of money that's paid to a professional before the job begins. This is usually non-refundable.

- **Developmental Editing** - An editing process to correct big problems with the text.

- **Discount** - The amount that retailers (bookstores) save off of the "List Price," if they wish to purchase a book from a wholesaler or distributor.

- **Distribution** - The mechanism by which a book gets from the publisher to a retailer.

- **Distributor** - A company that takes books from publishers and sells them to bookstores.

- **Epub** - The most common digital book (e-book) file type. The .epub file type is used by almost all digital book retailers, except for Amazon.com, which uses their own .mobi file type.

- **Gutter** - The white space (margin) between the inside edge of the open book's text and the center of the book. Careful! Sometimes this word is used to mean the total space of both pages (left and right) combined, and sometimes it refers to the distance of a single page.

- **Interior Design** - The process of creating a digital file of the insides of the book, including the title pages and book text, to be sent to the printer for printing.

- **ISBN** - International Standard Book Number. The number that all professionally published books must carry to be sold in a bookstore.

- **LCCN** - Library of Congress Control Number (previously Library of Congress Card Number). A unique number assigned to a title by the Library of Congress (LOC) for tracking, organizing and cataloging all books produced in the United States.

- **Line Editing** - Same as "Copy Editing."

- **List Price** - The suggested price of the book.

- **Margin** - The distance between the edge of the text and edge of the page.

- **Page Count** - The total number of pages in a book,

including non-numbered pages like the title page and copyrights. Careful! If your half-title page isn't page one, the page count will be different from the number on the last page of your book.

- **PDF** - The most common, reliable and permanent file type for delivering artwork and design files to your printer. PDFs are generally not editable after they are created.

- **Proofreading** - The process of checking for last-minute mistakes, like typos.

- **Recto** - The front of a page, or the right side page of an open book. The opposite is "Verso."

- **Returnable** - Denotes whether a retailer can return unsold copies of a book.

- **Source Files** - The files that were used to create a design document. Final documents are usually delivered as PDFs, which are not editable. Source files allow changes to be made and new PDFs to be generated.

- **Spine Height** - The thickness of the book.

- **Style Guide** - A book of rules for grammar, word usage and abbreviations. Examples include Associated Press (AP), The Chicago Manual of Style and MLA.

- **Typesetting** - The act of arranging words on a page for a printer. Part of the Interior Design Process.

- **Verso** - The back of a page, or the left side page of an open book. The opposite is "Recto."

Columbus Publishing Lab

The thing that separates Columbus Publishing Lab from all other self-publishing services is that we understand who the real customer is, and it's not you. We understand that we're helping you produce books for real readers, and that's who counts.

At Columbus Publishing Lab, we don't work in illusions. Our job isn't to convince you that you're getting a great self-publishing package, our job is to help you produce a professional book for real people to buy and read. We'll assess your satisfaction a year from now when your sales numbers come in.

Columbus Publishing Lab offers a variety of editorial, design, distribution and marketing services for authors who would like to self-publish. Our services are so good that several small presses also use our editorial and design teams to produce their books.

Self-publishing is always a risky endeavor. Most authors who self-publish do not recover their costs. But it's true that most authors who self-publish are getting ripped off by the big self-publishing companies and are way over-paying, or they're doing things themselves and the materials ultimately suffer. While we can't guarantee that you'll be profitable if you use our services, we can guarantee that your odds of success are much higher with one of our fairly-priced self-publishing packages than with most other avenues available to you.

At Columbus Publishing Lab, we don't just crank your manuscript through our machine and call whatever comes out the other side a "book." Instead, we connect your project with professional editors, designers and consultants who take an interest in your book and help to produce the best product possible. We don't use stock templates for our books, each one is carefully considered by a designer and something unique and effective is created just for you.

And we can do all of this at honest, affordable prices. You keep all of the rights to your book, at all times.

If you decide that self-publishing is right for you, I hope that you'll consider using Columbus Publishing Lab. I think you'll be glad that you did.

Learn more about Columbus Publishing Lab at
www.ColumbusPublishingLab.com

Brad Pauquette

Brad Pauquette lives in Columbus, Ohio with his wife and two sons.

Since 2008, he's worked as a marketing specialist, publishing consultant and editor, helping *New York Times* bestselling authors, professional athletes, and all sorts of writers, understand the publishing world, make good choices and produce great literature.

In 2009, Brad founded Columbus Creative Cooperative (CCC), a writers' resource and independent publisher in Columbus, Ohio. CCC strives to help writers produce great content and improve their writing.

Brad launched Columbus Press, an independent publisher of great fiction and narrative non-fiction, in 2013. While still in its infancy, the publisher has produced a number of well-received titles.

Despite his love of doing things himself and helping others pursue their goals, Brad still dreams of one day being a full-time, traditionally-published author himself. His novelette, *Sejal: The Walk for Water*, is his first published book.

Learn more about Brad at www.BradPauquette.com.

CPSIA information can be obtained
at www.ICGtesting.com
Printed in the USA
FFOW03n1842161115
18598FF